Enchanting MALAYSIA

DAVID BOWDEN

JOHN BEAUFOY PUBLISHING

Above: Traditional Malaysian dance is an important part of the culture and can be seen in many parts of the country.

Right: Small fishing villages can still be found especially along the East Coast of Peninsular Malaysia.

Contents

Above: Colonial architecture is evident in places such as the Royal Selangor Club in central Kuala Lumpur.

Opposite: Eclectic architectural styles are a feature of Kuala Lumpur as shown in the contrast between the traditional Sultan Abdul Samad Building and the modern Dayabumi Complex.

Title page: The Hotel Pullman Putrajaya Lakeside in the country's administrative capital.

Chapter 1: A Wealth of Diversity

Malaysia is a tropical Asian country that includes Peninsular Malaysia (also known as West Malaysia) and the East Malaysian states of Sarawak and Sabah located on the island of Borneo. The country straddles the Equator and covers an area of 333,000 sq km (127,413 square miles) with the peninsula accounting for 40 per cent of the landmass, Sabah 23 per cent and Sarawak 37 per cent.

There are 13 Malaysian states as well as the federal territories of Labuan (an island off Sabah's west coast and an offshore financial centre), Putrajaya (the planned administrative centre near Kuala Lumpur) and Kuala Lumpur (the capital).

To many visitors, there is a perception that much of Malaysia is covered in luxuriant tropical rainforests. While there certainly are large tracts of primary forests in places like the Titiwangsa Range and the 434,300-ha (173,720-acre) Taman Negara National Park – both in Peninsular Malaysia – the landscape is, in fact, much more varied ranging from high-density urbanized areas, such as the capital city, to remote island specks in the waters surrounding the country.

Malaysia is a vibrant destination that retains many elements of its diverse culture while having cities as modern as anywhere else in Asia. The people of Malaysia are open and interested in foreigners and as such are welcoming and friendly. They are justifiably proud of the wonderful range of dining delights in the country and more than happy to share a meal with visitors.

It is Malaysia's blend of multiculturalism and natural areas from beaches to islands, mountains and rainforests that make it such a popular Asian holiday destination for travellers of all kinds. This diverse landscape combined with its unique plants and animals offers tourists enchanting opportunities and a truly Asian experience.

Above: Kuala Lumpur has changed dramatically in its short history with contemporary skyscrapers like the Petronas Twin Towers now dominating the skyline.

Left: The different religious buildings from mosques and temples to churches are an obvious feature of multicultural Malaysia. Sree Maha Mariammam Temple in Penang is a typical Hindu place of worship.

Geography

Malaysia is located just north of the Equator and therefore has an equatorial climate (warm and wet). Monsoon winds influence most of the country but different parts are affected throughout the year – the northeast monsoon brings rain to the East Coast from November to March and the southwest monsoon results in rain along the West Coast from May to September.

Below: Many beaches, such as the ones on Redang Island, live up to their reputation as an island paradise.

Malaysia is one of the ten countries forming the Association of Southeast Asian Nations (ASEAN) and is bordered by Thailand, Singapore, Brunei, Indonesia and the Philippines. It also fronts some of the world's major stretches of water including the Straits of Malacca and the South China, Sulu and Celebes Seas.

The highest peaks in each part of the country are Mount Kinabalu in Sabah (4,101 m/13,455 ft), Mount Murud in Sarawak (2,423 m/7,946 ft) and Mount Tahan on the peninsula (2,187 m/7,175 ft). The climatic conditions in these and other mountainous areas are significantly cooler than the lowlands. A fact which lead to mountain retreats being built here in Malaya's colonial past, many of which are still in existence.

Rivers are another important geographical feature as they were once the only means of accessing certain parts of

the country. In some regions of East Malaysia they are still the best way into and out of the interior. Sarawak's Rajang River at 563 km (1,847 miles) is the longest in the country with the Kinabatangan in Sabah being the second longest at 560 km (1,837 miles).

Various island groups are also vital to the Malaysian tourism industry, most being lined with idyllic sandy beaches while others support pockets of wetlands.

Left: Along parts of the coastline, mangrove forests protect the foreshore as well as being an important habitat for bird and marine life.

Above: The country's highest peak, Mount Kinabalu.

History

Malaysia's strategic location along the great maritime trade routes between the West and East meant that early history was influenced by commerce. Goods from China and India passed through the country principally via the Straits of Malacca. Melaka (also spelt Malacca) developed in the 15th century to become one of the most strategic ports in the world. It has been surpassed these days by much larger ports but the old historic buildings offer a wonderful window onto the past.

In 1824 the East India Company took control of Singapore which, together with Melaka and Penang, became known as the Straits Settlements. Other Peninsular Malay states eventually came under British influence.

The present-day East Malaysian states of Sarawak and Sabah have a different history. While regional trade existed for centuries, the European colonial powers only became interested in Borneo in the more recent past. In 1841, English adventurer James Brooke was appointed Rajah of Sarawak by the Sultan of Brunei. The British North Borneo Company (an administrative organization) acquired trading concessions in present-day Sabah in 1881. Natural resources were exploited under British rule with tin mining and rubber plantations leading the economic growth.

After Japanese occupation during World War II, an independence movement gained momentum and the new nation of Malaysia was established on August 31, 1957. In 1963 both Sarawak and Sabah became part of Malaysia.

Malaysia is ruled by a King or Yang di-Pertuan Agong who is elected by the state sultans on a rotational basis every three years. The official residence is the new Istana Negara located near the centre of Kuala Lumpur on Jalan Duta. The King's role is mostly ceremonial and a democratically elected government has ensured political stability since independence.

Left: Malaysia's new Istana Negara or Royal Palace is the official residence of the King.

Above: Malaysia's flag has red and white stripes and a blue patch with a golden star and crescent. Each of the 13 states has its own flag.

Opposite: Islamic architecture is evident in many historic buildings, such as the Kuala Lumpur Railway Station.

The People

While Malaysia is multicultural, there are three main ethnic groups: Bumiputera (indigenous people including Malays), Chinese and Indian. The Bumiputera ('sons of the soil') include the Orang Asli, the forest-dwellers of Peninsular Malaysia, and some 32 East Malaysian ethnic communities.

Malaysia's multiculturalism is reflected in its art, music, food, crafts, customs and religious beliefs. It also leads to a colourful array of festivals with the major ones celebrated as national holidays. The main holidays are Hari Raya (marking the end of the Muslim fasting month), Chinese New Year, Deepavali (Hindu New Year), Wesak Day (a Buddhist celebration), Christmas Day and Merdeka Day (celebrating Malaysia's independence on August 31). Dates for some of these vary each year – the Tourism Malaysia website (see page 78) is the best source for actual dates as well as all other tourism events.

While most festivals are celebrated by specific ethnic groups or religions, Malaysia adopts a policy called 'open house' as a major part of the festivities. This means those celebrating often open their house to their friends and provide food and beverages. Even the Prime Minister has an open house to which everyone is invited.

Above left: *Being predominantly Muslim, mosques are a common sight on the Malaysian landscape.*

Above: *This Iban man is from one of many ethnic communities living in East Malaysia.*

Left: Red is an important colour for the Chinese as it symbolizes good luck.

Below: Malaysia has many festivals. Some of the Chinese celebrations feature giant incense sticks as part of the festivities.

Malaysia's main religions are Islam, Buddhism, Taoism, Christianity, Hinduism, Confucianism and Sikhism. While Islam is the largest, religious freedom is practised and in some parts of Malaysia, like Jalan Tokong (formerly Temple Street) in Melaka, places of worship of different religions are located close to each other: Kampung Keling Mosque and the Hindu Sri Poyyatha Vinayagar Moorthi Temple co-exist here and the famous Christ Church is nearby.

Ethnic diversity is also reflected in the variety of languages spoken. Visitors can sit in coffee shops and hear several languages or have discussions with locals who could lapse into three languages in the one sentence. Bahasa Malaysia is the official language and the one most Malaysians speak. Malaysians of Chinese heritage will also speak at least one Chinese dialect be it Teochew, Hakka, Foochow, Hokkien, Cantonese or Hainanese. Many Malaysians of Indian descent speak Tamil. When the languages spoken by the Orang Asli and those of the ethnic communities in East Malaysia are included, Malaysia becomes a country of great linguistic complexity. However, visitors soon discover that English is widely spoken, especially in urban areas, making travel easy.

Malaysian crafts are important in the culture. Many Malaysians wear *batik* and in East Malaysia, woven cotton called *pua kumbu* is worn by some tribal groups. Beadwork and pewter make excellent souvenirs. For leisure activities, kite flying, top-spinning, a self-defence sport called *silat* and shadow puppets called *wang kulit* are still popular.

Below: *A traditional Malaysian kite is called a 'wau'. They can be very complex in design and large in size and are still flown in some parts of the country. A popular version is the 'wau bulan' or moon-shaped kite that is also the symbol of Malaysia Airlines.*

Right: *Batik is a textile produced by using wax and dyes to create colourful patterns. Malaysian batik was adapted from Javanese techniques.*

The country has built on its history and traditions while forging into the 21st century. While many Malaysians uphold these traditions in their dress, religion and family ties, there are just as many who feel at home with the latest technology, global fashions and international lifestyle concepts. Many Malaysians enjoy shopping at the local *pasar malam* (night market) as well as in contemporary shopping malls lined with recognizable global brands. They will gladly enjoy a *teh tarik* (local tea) one day and a *caffè latte* in a branded Western coffee outlet the next. Malaysians enjoy their local hawker stall food while urban sophisticates will also seek out global cuisines complemented by international wines.

Malaysia is a developing economy with a population of 28.4 million people and a government implementing policies directed to attaining developed nation status. It is economically one of the most important regional economies and the 26th largest GDP in the world. While the services and industrial sectors are rapidly growing, a large percentage of the population still live a rural existence. Tin and rubber were once the mainstays of the economy but now petroleum and gas, palm oil, manufacturing, forestry, electronics, chemicals, semi conductors and tourism are all important foreign exchange earners. The Malaysian Ringgit is the official currency.

Left: The night market or 'pasar malam' is a popular place for Malaysians to shop for fresh produce, snacks, clothes and everyday items.

Above: Malaysians proudly display their national flag especially on National Day, August 31

Food

Malaysians live to eat and the most frequent greeting in the country is: *sudah makan* (have you eaten)? If the person has, the conversation will be about what they had. If not, there will be the suggestion that everyone should go and eat. In many cases, eating means snacking and many Malaysians eat five small meals of breakfast, lunch, tea, dinner and supper each day.

The main food styles follow the country's racial groups of Malay, Chinese and Indian but within these three main styles there's an infinite number of variations, such as northern and southern Indian, Malay food from the various states and Chinese food from almost every province in that country. Malaysians will swear by whoever produces the most famous version of a specific dish and will gladly go out of their way to seek out such renowned locations when travelling around the country.

This is exciting news for visitors as no-one will run out of something new to sample at almost every meal. Meals can be taken in simple but atmospheric hawker stalls through to sophisticated five-star restaurants. Some well-known dishes include: *laksa* (spicy noodle soup), *won ton*

This page: *Open-air, streetside eating in hawker stalls is common and satay is available in most.*

mee (noodles with meat dumplings), *mee goreng* (fried noodles), *nasi kandar* (rice smorgasbord), *roti canai* (flat, fried bread), *satay* (charcoal grilled meat on skewers) and *bak kut teh* (pork rib herbal soup). Sweet 'stretched' tea called *teh tarik* is Malaysia's own tea *cappuccino*.

Spices, chilli and *belancan* (shrimp paste) are important ingredients in many Malaysian dishes and while some are hot and spicy, others are not. One of the distinctive culinary styles in Malaysia is Nyonya (or Peranakan) which evolved when Chinese food was combined with Malay ingredients.

Durian is a football-sized, spiky, yellow-green fruit with a thick husk that's known as 'the king of fruits'. It 'tastes like heaven but smells like hell' and most Malaysians relish the durian season which typically runs from June to August although imported fruit from neighbouring nations extends the season almost year-round.

Above: Barbecued fish cooked over sizzling charcoal is sold in most markets.

Above left: Dishes of rice and noodles come in various forms from hawker plates to elaborate restaurant versions like this 'mee goreng'.

Left: Exotic tropical fruits are plentiful.

Unique Habitats

When Malaysia first began to trade with the outside world most of the country was covered in dense rainforest. Today, the most widely distributed vegetation, dipterocarp forest, is slowly being converted to urban areas, agriculture and plantations but an estimated 59 per cent of the country still has green cover. Not surprisingly, rainforest thrives in Malaysia because of the abundant sunlight and the hot, wet climate. These rainforests are tens of millions of years old and some of the most ancient in the world. Other major forest types include freshwater and mangrove swamp, peat swamp, limestone hills and montane. Secondary forests replace primary forests when the latter has been logged for its fine timber.

Above: Mangrove seeds are buoyant enabling them to float over long distances before finding a suitable mudflat on which to lodge and root.

Right: Lowland dipterocarp forest grows in a variety of habitats from water-lined lakes to hilly terrain.

Opposite: Many forests like those at the Rainforest Discovery Centre in Sepilok, Sabah, are accessible to visitors by a network of bridges and trails.

Various habitats remain in their pristine state and are protected as national parks, reserves and sanctuaries. These are important for the many animals that call Malaysia home. Malaysia is one of 12 mega diverse countries with 166,500 species, including 12,500 species of flowering plants.

Dipterocarp Forests

Dipterocarp forests occur naturally in Malaysian lowlands below 900 m (2,952 ft). The name is derived from the fact that the many seeds of these forest trees have two wings. The forest type is further divided into lowland (below 300 m/984 ft) and hill dipterocarp forest between 900 and 300 m (2,952 and 984 ft). According to WWF-Malaysia (World Wide Fund for Nature), pockets of lowland forests occur near Kuala Lumpur in the Sungai Buloh Reserve, Kanching Forest Reserve (including Templer's Park) and the Ampang Forest Reserve. Beautiful and relatively undisturbed forests can also be found at Taman Negara (Peninsular Malaysia), Mulu National Park (Sarawak) and in the Maliau Basin, Sepilok Forest Reserve and Danum Valley in Sabah. Conservation of these forests is important in order to maintain the nation's biodiversity as well as to provide opportunities for ecotourists.

Mangrove and Freshwater Swamp Forests

Mangrove swamp forests line many parts of coastal Malaysia. Specialized plants such as mangroves adapt to saline conditions. Mangroves not only protect the coastline from erosion and tsunami damage but also are vitally important as spawning grounds for fish and crustaceans.

Nipa palm forest replaces the mangroves as the water becomes less saline. Freshwater forests are regularly inundated by mineral-rich fresh water. Sabah's Kinabatangan River is home to this type of forest in which can be found

Orang-utans, Bornean Pygmy Elephants and Proboscis Monkeys. Peat swamp forest is a type of freshwater forest that once covered large tracts of the country with representative stands in Sarawak. In states like Johor, however, much of it has been cleared for plantations and agriculture.

Limestone Hill Forests

Limestone hills and outcrops are common features of the landscape from north of Kuala Lumpur into Thailand and especially Mount Mulu in Sarawak. Known as *karst* topography, they only occupy a small part of Malaysia's landmass but have high biodiversity and support many unique plants. Part of the karst topography includes the subterranean limestone cave systems, such as those found in Sarawak's Mulu National Park.

Montane Forests

There are two distinct types of montane forests: those between 1,200 and 1,700 m (3,937 and 5,557 ft) and upper montane, heath-like forest restricted to even higher peaks. Two forest storeys exist in the former and the tree height rarely exceeds 20 m (66 ft). In upper montane forests the vegetation becomes very stunted and gnarled due to the cool weather conditions. Soils here are acidic and the trees are covered with mosses, liverworts, epiphytes and lichens. These forests are made more atmospheric by the continual blanket of moist mists and clouds.

Climbers who ascend Sabah's Mount Kinabalu will experience both types of montane forest. At 1,200 m (3,937 ft) the lowland forest peters out and is replaced by oaks and conifers. The vegetation becomes sparser and lower in height with altitude; mosses are more common due to the cooler weather conditions. Orchids are a feature at this and higher altitudes. Rhododendrons appear but in the sub-alpine zone of the mountain only heath-like plants survive; most plant life cannot grow in the harsh climatic conditions.

Marine Environments

Malaysia is also home to many coral reefs most of which are associated with islands. Sipadan Island is one of the world's ten best diving locations but there are many other great diving sites including the reefs around Perhentian, Tioman, Redang, Kapas and Tenggol Islands. The Coral Triangle between the Philippines, Borneo and Indonesia is one of the world's richest in terms of marine diversity.

Opposite: The understorey of lowland dipterocarp forest is generally sparse although can be quite dense when light penetrates the canopy.

Below: Beaches are usually fringed with palms and casuarina trees.

Unique Plants

Malaysia's forests support many unique plants that thrive under climatic conditions ranging from hot and moist in the rainforests to cool and dry in some montane areas. The plants range in size from unicellular algae up to trees, like the *tualang* or *menggaris* (*Koompassia excelsa*), that can attain heights of 80 m (260 ft) and emerge above the canopy. Some plants that survive in the rainforests are extremely ancient, such as the cycads. These 'living fossils' first appeared on earth almost 280 million years ago.

Above: Malaysia is home to over 650 fern species with tree ferns like this having leaves as long as 4 m (13 ft).

Above right: Colourful orchids are a feature of Malaysian forests.

Malaysia is one of the most diverse floristic regions in the world. While tree species dominate the rainforest, other plant forms, such as vines, stranglers, shrubs, epiphytes, orchids and non-vascular plants also thrive here. There are some 8,500 flowering plant species in Peninsular Malaysia and 12,000 on Borneo; Mount Kinabalu alone is home to 33 per cent of the known plant species on Borneo.

Malaysia is also the meeting point for the floristic zones of Australia and continental Asia. Identified and named after celebrated naturalist Alfred Russel Wallace, the 'Wallace Line', which lies to the east of Borneo, separates Asian plant types from those exhibiting Australian features.

The easiest places to see Malaysia's unique flora are in national parks and forest reserves. Visitors to Peninsular Malaysia do not have to travel far from the capital to experience the rainforest as the Forest Research Institute Malaysia (FRIM) is located on the northern outskirts of Kuala Lumpur. Primary rainforest thrives here and a good trail network enables access to many rainforest features. Other places on the peninsula where forests remain intact are Royal Belum Nature Park, Endau Rompin National Park and Taman Negara.

Meanwhile, Borneo is considered a hotspot of world diversity and home to one of the largest variety of plants in the world. Rainforests in East Malaysia are home to many unusual plants such as *Alocasia macrorrhiza* which, at 3 m (10 ft) long and 1.9 m (6¼ ft) wide, has the biggest leaves in the world.

More than 50 species of pitcher plants (*Nepenthes* spp) grow in Malaysia. Using a leaf modified as a pitcher, insects are trapped and their nutrients are absorbed by the plant.

Of the 25,000 orchids known worldwide, 850 are found in Peninsular Malaysia and 2,500 in East Malaysia. Such is the richness of biodiversity in Kinabalu National Park that 1,200 orchid species have been recorded here alone. Rothschild's Slipper Orchid, a Kinabalu endemic, is considered the king of the slipper orchids.

Rafflesia are parasitic plants that grow on *Tetrastigma* vines. The largest is *R. arnoldii* from the neighbouring island of Sumatra with flowers of up to 100 cm (39 inches) in diameter. Blooms are rare and short-lived with two of the best places to see them being in Sabah in Kinabalu Park and the Rafflesia Centre near Tambunan.

Wild gingers are a common understorey plant in dipterocarp forests, especially along shaded gullies and stream beds.

Top: Pitcher plants secrete a liquid attractive to insects and which eventually digests them.

Above: Rafflesia flowers have a carrion-like stench that attracts flies for pollination.

Right: Most gingers flowers are vibrantly coloured and easily seen on the forest floor.

Unique Animals

Malaysia is home to many animal species though deforestation and agricultural clearing has partly reduced some animal habitats with the Orang-utan, Bornean Pygmy Elephant, Clouded Leopard, Malayan Tiger and Sumatran Rhinoceros considered endangered.

Orang-utans are naturally a big tourist draw and there are several wild areas and rehabilitation centres where they can be observed. Rehabilitation centres, such as Sepilok (Sabah) and Matang (Sarawak), are where orphaned animals are taught jungle survival before they are reintroduced into the forest. Wild Orang-utans may be seen in the Kinabatangan, Danum Valley and Tabin Wildlife Reserves in Sabah as well as in Batang Ai in Sarawak.

One of the most unusual monkeys in Borneo is the Proboscis Monkey, the males of which have pendulous noses and barrel bellies. Other primates include the Silvered-leaf Monkey, Pig-tailed Macaque, Red-leaf

Monkey, Long-tailed Macaque, Agile Gibbon, Slow Loris and Western Tarsier.

The Sun Bear is the world's smallest bear, mostly nocturnal, found in lowland forests and named after the light patch on its chest. The largest cat is the Malayan Tiger. Its stripes provide camouflage in the dappled light of the forest understorey. Forests are also home to the Pangolin (ant eater), Gaur (or Seladang), Asian Elephant (found in Peninsular Malaysia), Clouded Leopard, Malayan Tapir and the now very rare Sumatran Rhino in Borneo. The Bornean Pygmy Elephant, restricted to Borneo, is smaller than the Asian Elephant. Other important animals that aren't always in the wildlife limelight are bats, deer, shrews, rodents, porcupines, pigs, wild cats and squirrels.

Above: Adult Malayan Tigers average 2.6 m (8 $\frac{1}{2}$ feet) in length.

Left: This female adult Gaur is lighter in colour than the black male.

Opposite left: Habitat destruction is threatening the survival of the Orang-utan.

Opposite right: The Proboscis Monkey is named because of its long nose.

Left: The Green Crested Lizard (Bronchocela cristatella) is commonly found in primary and secondary rainforest as well as urban gardens and parklands.

Below: Sunbirds drink nectar from colourful flowers.

While seeking wildlife in its natural state isn't easy due to animals being camouflaged and the density of the vegetation, places like Taman Negara, Kinabatangan River, Danum Valley and Mulu National Park are some of the best locations to start. Visitors need to be patient and while most wish to see the better-known larger species, it's often the smaller ones that are seen, such as the insects, bats, reptiles, spiders, amphibians and butterflies. In a study in Borneo 3,000 different insect species were collected in one tree. The Atlas Moth, the world's largest moth with a wing span of 25 cm (9 in), is found in Malaysia. Other noteworthy

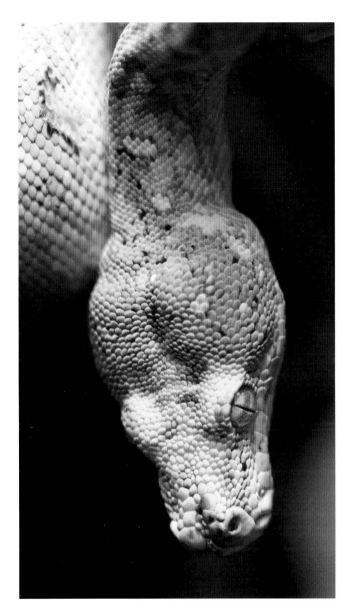

insects include Rajah Brookes Birdwing, considered one of the world's most beautiful butterflies. The large rhinoceros beetle has menacing horns and can lift 850 times its own weight. Stick insects confuse predators by mimicking the twigs they live on. Some insects live in colonies and play an important role in decomposing forest detritus into soil. Marching ants are known to invade the forest floor by swarming across it as an army would to battle. Caves are another habitat that, although dark, are swarming with life.

Bird-watching in Malaysia is rewarding with 656 species having been recorded in Peninsular Malaysia and 669 on the island of Borneo. Malaysia is on the flight path for migratory birds from eleven nations. Nine species of hornbill can be found in Malaysia – Rhinoceros, Plain-pouched, Wreathed, Helmeted, Wrinkled, Oriental Pied, Asian Black, White-crowned and Bushy-crested. They have unique nesting characteristics where the female is sealed in a tree hollow and fed by the male through a hole.

The Reticulated Python of South-East Asia is typical of many tropical fauna in being well camouflaged. It can grow to 10 m (33 ft) making it the world's largest snake and can digest large animals including mammals. There are many other reptiles and amphibians including turtles, crocodiles, snakes, lizards and frogs.

However, not all Malaysian fauna is land-based – the coral reefs around Sabah are some of the most species-rich in the world.

Left: The Freshwater False Gharial (Tomistoma schlegelii) is rare but can be found in some Malaysian lakes.

Above left: While not venomous, large pythons are dangerous since they are constrictors.

Land and Resources

Forests have important ecotourism value although logging occurs in some areas and makes a valuable contribution to the economy. As well as being vital for the ecological well-being of the forests, there are many economically important plants that grow naturally here. Trees are logged as a source of timber for furniture, flooring and other uses within the construction industry.

Palms grow widely throughout Malaysia with over 400 identified species. Rattan is one of the most commercially important plants as it is used extensively for making furniture as well as being used in the construction industry. Palms are also used as building materials (*nipa* is still used for thatching on many traditional homes). Fruit trees like durian, mangosteen and rambutan are important and large numbers of plants have medicinal value.

Left: *Originally imported from Brazil, the rubber tree is an important cash crop in Malaysia.*

Above: *Much lowland forest has been cleared for extensive oil palm plantations.*

Left: Tea plantations are a feature of the Cameron Highlands and the slopes of Mount Kinabalu.

Below: Oil is extracted and refined off the East Coast of Peninsular Malaysia, Sabah and Sarawak.

Many Malaysians lead a rural existence with some remote communities in East Malaysia still practising shifting cultivation (a type of agriculture in which the cultivated area is regularly moved to allow the soil to recover naturally). Links with the outside world for many communities are along rivers which snake their way from the interior to the coast. Visitors who fly into Mulu National Park in Sarawak have the opportunity to see the Baram River which is one such vast meandering river.

On some of the floodplains through which these rivers flow, the primary forests are being converted to plantations that have always played an important role in the Malaysian economy. Rubber, oil palm, cocoa, tea and increasingly tree species, such as Acacia for paper production, are grown in single crop plantations which cover large tracts of land.

Padi fields of rice cover many parts of Malaysia, especially the 'rice bowls' of the northern states of Perlis and Kedah. Rice is important to the nation as it is a dietary staple for most Malaysians. Fishing is another important industry since fish is a vital source of protein for many. Fishing villages along the East Coast of the peninsula in particular are very picturesque.

Off the coasts of Terengganu (Peninsular Malaysia),

Sarawak and Sabah, petroleum and liquefied natural gas make valuable contributions to the economy. Malaysia is a nett exporter of both with the national oil company Petronas providing 30% of the federal budget.

The manufacturing and service sectors of the economy are also important to the national productivity. Trade free zones in Penang and Cyberjaya, Malaysia's 'Silicon Valley' to the south of Kuala Lumpur, help attract direct foreign investment into the economy.

Adventures, Sport and Lifestyle

In addition to the many festivals and cultural activities celebrated throughout Malaysia there are a great many recreational and sporting pursuits for visitors, whether as participants or spectators.

The most prestigious sporting event, attracting enthusiasts from around the world, is the Petronas Malaysia F1 Grand Prix staged annually at the modern Sepang International Circuit located near Kuala Lumpur International Airport (KLIA). The track also hosts other major international events, such as the MotoGP bike race.

At the end of the year international attention focuses on the waters off Terengganu on Malaysia's East Coast where the Monsoon Cup is contested. The normally tranquil waters off Duyong Island and the mouth of the Terengganu River are whipped up during the monsoon season to guarantee some spirited sailing during the 'Formula One of Sailing'. This is a match race regatta involving professional crews from around the world who all compete in Foundation 36 racing yachts. Duyong Island is the home of a traditional wooden boat building industry but it has been transformed into an international resort and marina development with repair facilities for all types of leisure boat.

There are several other yacht races as well as marinas in various locations for those who want some non-competitive sailing. Langkawi with its four marinas is the best serviced. The most established Malaysian yacht race is the nine-day Raja Muda Selangor International Regatta that ends in Langkawi. It starts from Port Klang near Kuala Lumpur and includes three overnight passages and day races off Penang and Langkawi. This challenging 445 km (240 nautical miles) race is keenly contested on the water but is also known for its friendly camaraderie.

Left: The tropical waters of Malaysia are ideal for sailing and a dozen or so marinas provide berths for ocean-going yachts.

Opposite: Climbing the world's highest 'via ferrata' is just one of many challenges that awaits adventurous travellers. 'Via ferrata' is Italian for 'iron road' and describes a series of cables, ladders and bridges near the summit of Malaysia's highest mountain, Mount Kinabalu.

Right: For many Malaysians a round of golf on one of the many courses throughout the country is their most rewarding sporting activity. Courses like the Meru Valley Golf and Country Club in Ipoh also provide accommodation in forested surroundings.

Opposite: Outdoor music festivals over several days have now become annual events on the tourism calendar. The Rainforest World Music Festival staged near Kuching in Sarawak every July is one of the region's most acclaimed and showcases local indigenous music plus the electrical sounds of internationally-renowned artistes.

The sport which most Malaysians are fanatical about is football (soccer) and while the national team is well supported, international matches from all the major football leagues are beamed into most coffee shops and bars around the country. Almost every village will have a football field and visitors are always welcome to join in.

In 1998 Kuala Lumpur hosted the Commonwealth Games and many impressive new facilities were constructed. While many Malaysians participate in sports, the climate makes the playing of some outdoor activities more demanding, so indoor sports like squash and badminton are very popular. A sport that is unique to the region is *sepak takrow*, a kind of volleyball played using the feet rather than the hands.

Running, cycling and triathlons (swimming, running and cycling) are growing in popularity throughout Malaysia. The Tour de Langkawi Malaysia is an international cycling event staged every February. Running events like the Penang Bridge International Marathon every November attract an international field.

Many visitors to Mount Kinabalu in Sabah make the two-day climb or participate in more adventurous activities such as ascending the 'Via Ferrata' (a route supported by manmade cables, bridges and ladders) up the mountain.

Each October, the Kinabalu International Climbathon attracts runners who race to the summit and back, the current record for which is two hours, 33 minutes. Other mountains to conquer include Sarawak's Mount Mulu 2,376 m (7,795 ft), Mount Ledang 1,276 m (4,186 ft) on the Melaka and Johor border and the nine-day jungle ascent on Mount Tahan in Taman Negara 2,187 m (7,175 ft).

Jungle trekking, white-water rafting and bird-watching are other activities that lure tourists to inland Malaysia. With some 265 golf courses from beachside links courses to those high up in the mountains, golf here challenges many players with course diversity and is attractive due to its value-for-money green fees.

Recreational watersports are plentiful in most coastal and island resorts and bicycle hire is common. Parasailing is possible off beaches in Langkawi, Penang and Kota Kinabalu, while Hobie cat sailboats are available for hire in most island resorts. Scuba diving around the islands is world-class.

Tourists are also attracted to Malaysia for major music festivals such as the Rainforest World Music Festival held at the Sarawak Cultural Village in July, the Borneo Jazz Festival staged in Miri in May and Langkawi Live or the Penang International Jazz Festival every December.

Chapter 2: Peninsular Malaysia

Peninsular or West Malaysia extends from the border with Thailand in the north to the island state of Singapore in the south. The northernmost point is Padang Besar and the southernmost tip (and of the Asian mainland) is Tanjung Paia in southwest Johor. This is the most populous part of the country and the most urbanized and industrialized.

Peninsular Malaysia includes not only the Federal Territory of Kuala Lumpur but also the states of Selangor, Negeri Sembilan, Melaka, Johor, Pahang, Terengganu, Kelantan, Perak, Penang, Kedah and Perlis. The main cities are Kuala Lumpur (the capital), Johor Bahru, Kuantan, Kuala Terengganu, Kota Bharu, George Town and Ipoh as well as the new administrative centre of Putrajaya and Malaysia's Multimedia Super Corridor of Cyberjaya.

While both have their tourist charms, the East Coast is less developed than the West. Various island groups surround the coast including, on the East Coast, the Perhentians, Redang, Kapas, Tenggol, Tioman and the Johor Islands plus Pangkor, Penang and Langkawi on the West Coast. Most are resort islands with either simple chalets or, in the case of Pangkor, award-winning international resorts. They offer a variety of watersports with snorkelling and diving being the most popular activities.

In addition to the islands and cities, the principal tourist attractions are the Cameron Highlands, Fraser's Hill, Melaka, Genting Highlands and Taman Negara.

Right: Kuala Lumpur's contrasting architecture is best observed around Merdeka Square with its expanse of grass called the Padang where Malaysia's independence was proclaimed in 1957. The Sultan Abdul Samad Building with its white and copper domes is the city's most impressive Moorish-styled landmark. It was designed by A.C. Norman, a British architect who was also responsible for St Mary's Cathedral located opposite.

Above: Forested limestone hills and long sandy beaches like this one at Tanjung Rhu are two of the main reasons for tourists to travel to Langkawi situated off the northwest coast of the peninsula.

Left: At Aquaria KLCC there are 5,000 marine creatures and visitors can observe sharks and rays at close quarters in the glassed, walk-through tunnels.

Kuala Lumpur

First impressions are important: Kuala Lumpur's international airport with its modern facilities and its fast connections to the city by train or by a one-hour taxi ride down the freeway makes a good introduction to the country.

Situated in the Klang Valley, the capital city itself (often just shortened to KL) is a fascinating city with many interesting sights, culinary variety and excellent shopping. Though it has several older sections, it is actually one of Asia's youngest capitals. The discovery of tin at the confluence of the Gombok and Klang Rivers in 1857 lead to a settlement which has evolved into one of Asia's most vibrant, cosmopolitan cities. KL has made up for its youth and has seen meteoric growth over recent decades.

Above and left: Kuala Lumpur City Centre (KLCC) is a destination in itself with parklands surrounding the 88-storey Petronas Twin Towers. This is one of the world's tallest buildings and the world's tallest twin towers. One of the city's best nighttime views of the towers is from SkyBar on the 33rd floor of Traders Hotel

Opposite: The observation deck near the top of the 421-m (1,381-ft) high Kuala Lumpur Tower (a telecommunications mast) provides a great bird's-eye view of the city. At the base of the tower is a rainforest reserve with walking trails.

Right: Just to the east of Merdaka Square is the picturesque Jamek Mosque with its Moorish domes, pink and white archways, and tall minarets matched by those on KL's old Railway Station to the south (see page 9).

Above left: The Minangkabau-styled roof of the National Museum is a unique architectural style. Beneath the sweeping eaves, archaeological and ethnological displays are housed.

Left: The Lake Gardens is a large expanse of greenery that includes a Deer Park, Orchid Garden, Butterfly Park and Bird Park.

Above: The National Mosque with its pleated roofline and tall minarets is located on the edge of Lake Gardens. Nearby is the Islamic Arts Museum Malaysia which retains Islamic detailing while incorporating the functionality of a contemporary museum.

Putrajaya

The sheer scale of Malaysia's new federal administrative centre, Putrajaya, is a sight to behold. While the idea for a planned city was conceived just prior to the beginning of the 21st century, it has rapidly evolved into the pride of the nation. Many government departments have relocated here and residents enjoy an enhanced quality of life in an environment that is still rooted in Malaysian culture and tradition. It is located 25 km (15½ miles) to the southwest of Kuala Lumpur with several expressways leading there and then on to the airport. Its semi-rural setting makes it a pleasant weekend escape from the city.

Below: Putrajaya was designed as a 'city in a garden' with an emphasis on landscaping throughout. Extensive wetlands and a network of waterfront trails surround Putrajaya Lake.

Right: Putrajaya Botanical Gardens (Taman Botani) are home to a colourful display of tropical plants. Some 700 species from over 90 countries thrive in the 93-ha (230-acre) park.

Opposite: The green-domed Prime Minister's Department Building or 'Perdana Putra' is one of Putrajaya's most impressive buildings.

Left: Seri Wawasan Bridge crossing over Lake Putrajaya is typical of the many lakes and bridges that are a feature of Putrjaya's landscape.

Below: The palm-fringed foreshore of Lake Putrajaya provides a tropical setting adjacent to the five-star Pullman Putrajaya Lakeside Hotel

Selangor

Most international visitors to Malaysia arrive in Selangor state since the Kuala Lumpur International Airport (KLIA) is located here near Sepang and the F1 circuit. Selangor includes the state capital of Shah Alam and the KL satellite suburbs of Petaling Jaya and Subang Jaya. For visitors, the main attractions are the Sunway Lagoon, The Mines, the Kampung Kuantan fireflies and several forest reserves.

Top left: The skyline of Shah Alam, 20 km (12 miles) to the west of Kuala Lumpur is dominated by the magnificent Sultan Salahuddin Abdul Aziz Shah or Blue Mosque. This is the largest in South-East Asia and features an enormous dome.

Left: A fisherman crosses the Selangor river at sunset.

Above: Eco-adventurers can head to Kuala Selangor on the banks of the Selangor River. There a nature park is home to monkeys and migratory birds while in nearby Kampung Kuantan, boatman take visitors along the river each evening to see the thousands of flickering lights of fireflies that inhabit the riverine vegetation.

Right: Close to Kuala Lumpur there are forest trails in the Forestry Research Institute Malaysia (FRIM), Templer's Park and Kanching Forest Reserve.

Left and below: Batu Caves have a 272-step staircase that leads to a Hindu shrine inside a 100-m (328-ft) limestone cavem. They are located 13 km (8 miles) to the north of the city centre and are the focus for the colourful and energetic Thaipusam Hindu festival staged here at the beginning of each year. Playful monkeys also make this their home.

Northern Peninsular Malaysia

Head north from Kuala Lumpur to the states of Perak, Penang, Kedah and Perlis. The main cities and towns in Perak are Ipoh, Taiping and Kuala Kangsar; in Penang, George Town and Butterworth; and Kedah, Alor Star and Kangar in Perlis, all towns worth visiting, as well as Langkawi, the top island resort, the Pangkor Islands and the Royal Belum Forest Reserve.

Rolling limestone hills with subterranean caves are a feature of the topography. Rice fields north of Penang to the Thai border add colour to the landscape – verdant green during the growing phase and turning golden yellow just prior to harvesting.

Below: Ipoh flourished when tin was discovered here and there are several grand colonial buildings in town, the most impressive of which is the railway station.

Opposite: Ipoh is surrounded by limestone hills so typical of northwest Peninsular Malaysia. The vegetation that develops on limestone is species rich with 14% of all known species of flowering plants occurring on what is just 0.3% of Malaysia's land surface.

Above: The royal town of Kuala Kangsar features the old palace called Istana Kenangan which is now the Perak Royal Museum.

Left: Masjid Ubudiah with its distinctive golden domes is one of Kuala Kangsar's and Malaysia's most iconic buildings. This Moorish-style mosque was completed in 1917

Penang

Founded by Francis Light in 1786, Penang was the first British colony established in Malaysia. As a spice island Penang was very important for trade between Asia and Europe. It is mostly considered an island but the state actually has two parts – the island or Pulau Penang and the mainland centred on Butterworth. As well as touring the heritage architecture, dining is a great pleasure here: the *New York Times* rated Penang as having South-East Asia's liveliest street food scene.

Below: The Eastern and Oriental (E & O) Hotel was once considered 'the finest hotel east of the Suez'. It opened in 1885 and continues to offer elegant colonial ambiance and service.

Right: In 2008, parts of historic George Town on the mainland were inscribed on the UNESCO World Heritage List (a joint site together with Melaka) and tourism has since thrived.

This page: The UNESCO World Heritage zone of George Town is a warren of streets and passageways crammed with historic shop lots (above), temples, clan houses and mosques which can be admired while taking a trishaw ride. Visitors can watch traditional artisans, such as carvers, goldsmiths and joss-stick makers, at work. Heritage restoration is a feature with fine examples, such as Dr Sun Yat Sen's former house and Kapitan Keling Mosque on Armenian Street (left). Nearby, Khoo Kongsi Temple has been renovated while cafés, restaurants and heritage hotels have opened within some heritage buildings.

Above: Pinang Peranakan Mansion at 29 Church Street, George Town is the faithfully restored former home of a rich Baba (a Chinese man who married a local Malay woman). It operates as a Baba-Nyonya Museum to offer a glimpse of the many traditions and customs of this unique community.

Right: Cheong Fatt Tze Mansion, located in Leith Street, George Town was once the home of a wealthy Chinese businessman. It has been lovingly restored and now operates as a boutique hotel and is affectionately known as the 'Blue Mansion' for its striking azure-coloured exterior.

This page: Penang's beaches include the strip of bays and headlands stretching from Tanjung Bungah to Batu Ferringhi which is home to ten or so international resorts including the Parkroyal (right). All beachside resorts like the Shangri-La Rasa Sayang Resort and Spa (below) have restaurants, bars and spas. Many guests check in, chill out and do little else on the island.

Langkawi

Langkawi Island in the state of Kedah is considered Malaysia's premier island destination with facilities ranging from an international airport to duty-free shopping and including watersports, natural spaces, iconic restaurants and beachside bars.

Langkawi's successful holiday formula also includes its easy access by flight from Kuala Lumpur and Penang and a pace of life that is very relaxed. Added to this are several picturesque beaches including Pantai Cenang, Datai Bay and Pantai Tengah.

This is possibly the most complete island destination in the country as it offers a range of land and sea activities for all ages. Visitors can enjoy relaxing on the beaches, take a sunset cruise around the offshore islands or head off on a trek through the rainforest.

These pages: Stylish international resorts like the Sheraton, Westin (opposite, bottom left), Four Seasons (opposite top), The Datai, The Andaman, Tanjung Rhu (opposite, bottom right), Berjaya, Pelangi, Frangipani, Tanjung Sanctuary and Four Points add to Langkawi's appeal. These beachfront resorts offer restaurants, spas, bars and watersports. Boutique resorts like Bon Ton (top and right) and Temple Tree offer a uniquely Malaysian experience with their antique houses and contemporary interiors.

While Langkawi is best known for its sun, surf and sand, its natural attractions provide another dimension to this tropical island destination. No buildings along the beachfront rise above the height of a coconut tree and, when viewed from the air by planes approaching Langkawi International Airport, most of the islands are covered with vegetation. Parts of Langkawi are protected as a UNESCO Geopark (a valuable geological park).

Langkawi wetlands are particularly scenic as steep limestone walls rise from the mangrove-lined mudflats. They are home to various species of mangroves while rare cycads cling to the barren limestone surfaces seemingly defying the laws of natural development by growing in narrow crevices with limited soil.

Diving is best done in more distant waters than those around the main island. For diving enthusiasts, Pulau Payar Marine Park comprising four small coral islands just south of Langkawi is worth the journey. Coral gardens and fish of all colours abound in the clearer waters here. A large floating pontoon facility offers a complete day's activity for all the family and proves popular with those who come to snorkel near the safety of the pontoon.

Below: Langkawi's forests are home to wildlife, such as squirrels, flying lemurs, monkeys and a wealth of birdlife including hornbills. Monitor Lizards amble through the undergrowth while the rare Rainbow Lizard (pictured) scurries along the beaches.

Right: There are two mountains to explore – the taller, Gunung Raya and the more accessible, Gunung Machincang. A steep cable car ride to the summit of Machincang enables visitors to see as far as Thailand's Tarutao Marine Park on the horizon.

Left: Adventurous visitors can enjoy a thrilling journey through Langkawi's rainforest canopy.

Above: A variety of watersports ranging from parasailing to kayaking is possible in the waters surrounding Langkawi.

Left: Four marinas cater for sailing enthusiasts.

Southern Peninsular Malaysia

Heading south from Kuala Lumpur the highway passes through the states of Negeri Sembilan, Melaka and Johor with connections to neighbouring Singapore via two crossings over the Straits of Johor: the causeway in Johor Bahru and Tuas crossing in western Johor.

Port Dickson is a beach resort in Negeri Sembilan that is popular with locals as it is the closest beach to Kuala Lumpur. Melaka is the next state to the south followed by Johor which is mostly covered in oil palm plantations.

Iskandar Malaysia in the southernmost part of Johor is the country's first economic growth corridor and spans a development of 2,217 sq km (855 square miles) that includes manufacturing, residential, recreational and commercial components. The 31 ha (76 acre) theme park, Legoland Malaysia, is also to be found here.

Left: Seremban, the state capital of Negeri Sembilan, is 62 km (38 miles) south of Kuala Lumpur. Colonial-styled offices overlook the shady Lake Gardens and old Minangkabau-styled buildings with horn-shaped rooflines can be seen.

Below: The cultural complex and museum of Taman Seri Budaya in Seremban features an old wooden palace.

Opposite top: Johor's capital of Johor Bahru ('JB') is known as Malaysia's southern gateway. There are several old buildings in the capital with the former palace now housing the Sultan Abu Bakar Museum.

Opposite below: This bridge on the Senai to Desaru Expressway enables quick access to the southern beaches.

Melaka

Melaka (or Malacca) is a popular day visit destination from Kuala Lumpur but there are enough attractions and first-class accommodation to justify a visit of several days.

In 2008, parts of the historic town centre of Melaka were inscribed on the UNESCO World Heritage List (a joint site with George Town, Penang). The narrow streets are a living museum lined with traditional Chinese shop lots, where artisans still ply their trade.

Just south of Melaka in Ujong Pasir, a sunset meal in the Portuguese Village is highly recommended.

Above: *Ayer Keroh on the outskirts of the city is another tourism hub with a planetarium (pictured), Mini Malaysia (a park with models of 13 traditional houses), a nature reserve, a zoo and several resorts.*

Above right: *The highly decorated door of one of the Chinese clan associations in Malaysia.*

Right: *Visitors can admire Melaka's historic attractions by taking a river cruise.*

Left: Melaka's historic heart is dominated by several striking red buildings, such as Christ Church, dating back to the colonial era.

East Coast

Peninsular Malaysia's East Coast extends from the Straits of Johor in the south up to Thailand. Most people visit the states of Terengganu and Kelantan, although Mersing and Tanjung Leman in Pahang are departure ports for the Johor Islands and Tioman. Known as Malaysia's cultural heartland, the East Coast features long sandy beaches along the South China Sea, beautiful offshore islands, as well as sleepy fishing villages where residents are guided by traditional ways of life and there are fewer trappings of modernity.

Below: Kelantan's busy, four-storey Central Market (Pasar Besar Siti Khadijah) is the place to start exploring historic landmarks. Trishaw riders sit outside the front of the markets ready to take shoppers home or on to other sights, such as the Cultural Centre, Handicraft Village, Istana Jahar and the World War II Museum.

Opposite: Kampung Cina in central Kuala Terengganu is a significant historical site that supports a unique confluence of Malaysia's varied cultural heritage and includes the Istana Maziah, old Chinese shops (pictured) and Malay villages.

Below: The East Coast is sleepier with things moving at a slower pace to life on the West Coast. The Floating Mosque near Kuala Terengganu is one of the landmark buildings.

These pages: *The East Coast is perfect for relaxing holidays whatever the budget. Inexpensive chalets are situated in all areas especially Cherating while luxury resorts like Tanjong Jara near Dungun are also available. Club Med (opposite and left) at Cherating is very popular with families from around the globe. Wind and kite surfing are great sports to try on nearby Balok Beach (above).*

Islands

Hundreds of islands are dotted around the Malaysian coastline with the Langkawi group alone comprising 99. Many are small and undeveloped but others are popular holiday destinations. The main tourist islands are Perhentian, Redang, Kapas, Tenggol, Tioman and the Johor Islands (Rawa, Aur and Sibu) off the East Coast of the peninsula; Pangkor, Penang and Langkawi off the West Coast; and Sipadan, Mabul, Banggi, Turtle Islands, Lankayan, Layang Layang, Tunku Abdul Rahman National Park, Tiga and Labuan off Sabah.

Right and opposite: Tioman Island is a mostly undeveloped island in the South China Sea located off the port of Mersing in Johor. It has only one large resort with full facilities including a coastal golf course. In addition there are many simple chalets or the exclusive boutique resort of JapaMala (pictured). Tioman has a small airport with flights from Kuala Lumpur and Singapore while ferry services operate from the mainland.

This page: Two peaks rise above forest-covered Tioman Island with most of the chalets and small fishing villages on the western side. Diving, snorkelling and walking to the eastern side and back are the most popular pursuits here.

This page: Several island groups have a Robinson Crusoe setting with simple chalets rather than large resorts. Visitors to Lankayan Island off Sabah can step from their chalet right into the waters of the Sulu Sea (above). Chalets, eco-adventures, sailing and watersports on Malaysia's resort islands have helped put the country on the world's tourism map. Many visitors to these islands learn to dive at an accredited dive school or seek out fun activities like the banana boat rides at Pangkor (right).

Mountain Retreats

Malaysia has various mountainous regions. While these are mostly rugged and covered in impenetrable jungle, there are several east-west crossings over the central range of the peninsula as well as road access to some of the mountainous areas in East Malaysia, many of which were developed as hill stations during the colonial era and continue today as cool mountain resorts.

The best known hill stations are the Cameron Highlands and Fraser's Hill (Bukit Fraser). The other hill resorts include the Genting Highlands, Berjaya Hills, Bukit Larut (Maxwell Hill), Penang Hill, Mount Kinabalu (Sabah) and the Borneo Highlands (Sarawak).

Fraser's Hill located at 1,509 m (4,950 ft) is a two-hour drive north from Kuala Lumpur. It is a picturesque hill resort popular with golfers and bird-watchers. While it has some similar qualities to the Cameron Highlands, it is much smaller and appeals to those who appreciate the tranquillity of the cool hills away from the crowds.

This page: The largest and oldest hill station is the Cameron Highlands in Pahang situated at 1,783 m (5,850 ft). Its cool weather first appealed to heat-weary colonialists who took refuge here from the lowlands. Tudor-styled homes and hotels, cream teas and rose gardens provide a genteel ambiance. Tea plantations carpet the rolling hills and forest trails make this a refreshing retreat.

This page: The Genting Highlands (below) at an altitude of 2,000 m (6,560 ft) is an hour's drive from Kuala Lumpur. This mountain resort is home to Malaysia's only casino and an entertainment complex of theme parks (right), hotels, restaurants and shops. Berjaya Hills Resort at Bukit Tinggi in Pahang is close by. Situated at 823 m (2,700 ft), it includes the French-themed resort of Colmar Tropicale, Japanese gardens and tea rooms, accommodation, golf, horse-riding and spa treatments.

Taman Negara

Taman Negara (simply translated as National Park) is Malaysia's oldest and largest national park at 4,343 sq km (1,680 square miles). Established in 1939, the park is located on the peninsula with sections situated in the three states of Pahang, Terengganu and Kelantan. The most accessible part is in Pahang with the park headquarters at Kuala Tahan. While Kuala Tahan can be reached via a plantation road, most visitors depart from Kuala Tembeling and take a leisurely two-hour journey along the Tembeling River into the park.

These pages: Taman Negara was established to protect the fauna and various floristic communities including the lowland dipterocarp forests. These forests are home to over 600 bird species and some 200 mammals including the Tapir, Asian Elephant and Gaur as well as deer, squirrels, monkeys, gibbons and various cat species, such as the Malayan Tiger. Locating wildlife in the rainforest is not easy but journeys through the forest canopy or along remote rivers enable visitors to get closer to the animals.

Chapter 3: East Malaysia, Sarawak

Borneo includes the Malaysian states of Sarawak and Sabah as well as Brunei and Indonesian Kalimantan.

The island is home to some 30 ethnic groups but with six main groups – Barito, Bidayuh, Dusun-Kadazan-Murut, Iban, Kayan-Kenyah and Kelabit-Lun Bawang. These groups can be further divided into coastal and inland people (Dayaks) with those inland being highly tribalized but low in numbers. Many are hunter-gatherers or shifting cultivators, although development has partially affected traditional lifestyles.

Kuching and Beyond

Kuching, the capital of Sarawak, on the south-west coast is a gateway to various natural and cultural attractions ranging from national parks to longhouses, golf courses, dolphin watching and the beaches at Damai. Bako and Kubah National Parks are close to Kuching as are the Orang-utan centres of Matang and Semenggoh.

Miri in the far north is Sarawak's second city where Malaysia's first oil well was spudded in 1910. Today, drilling mostly occurs offshore but Miri remains an important service centre. While many transit here on the way to Mulu Caves and the interior, for those who stay there are pleasant beachside resorts and the Borneo Jazz Festival in May.

Above right: Kuching's new State Legislative Assembly Hall (in the background) dominates its Sarawak River location.

Right: Sarawak's Cultural Village near Damai Beach Resort is home to seven local communities.

Above: Kuching's Waterfront has been rejuvenated into gardens and recreational facilities and is recognized as one of Asia's finest public spaces. Sampans called 'tambang' ferry people across the river.

Left: Kuching's Sarawak Museum is considered one of the best in Asia. There are two sections each housing tribal artefacts and there is also a good natural history section.

Sarawak – Natural Places and Parks

Sarawak's Forestry Department administers 15 national parks (including Tanjung Datu, Kubah, Lambir Hills, Similajau, Loagan Bunut, Talang-Satang, Gunung Gading, Rajang Mangroves and Gunung Buda), five wildlife sanctuaries and five reserves. Some one million forested hectares (2,471,054 acres) or eight per cent of Sarawak are protected. These include archaeological sites, natural areas, animal habitats and wildlife rehabilitation centres. The four most visited national parks are: Bako, Batang Ai, Niah Caves and Gunung Mulu.

Top right: Batang Ai is located 250 km (155 miles) from Kuching in the southwest of Sarawak near the Kalimantan border. Some 24,000 ha (59,305 acres) of dipterocarp forest surround a lake formed when the river was dammed for hydro-electric generation. Stay in the Hilton Resort (pictured) or up-river in the eco-friendly Nanga Sumpa Lodge. Orang-utan, gibbons, monkeys, hornbills, deer and the Clouded Leopard may be sighted.

Below right: The 7,067 ha (17,463 acres) of Similajau National Park are home to gibbons and monkeys as well as crocodiles which inhabit the rivers. Visitors also travel from nearby Bintulu to this coastal national park to see some 185 bird species including seven species of hornbills.

Right: While Gunung Mulu National Park is named after its highest peak at 2,376 m (7,795 ft), it's the caves of this UNESCO World Heritage Site that are the biggest attraction. Most visitors fly from Miri to explore Deer, Lang, Wind and Clearwater Caves which are accessible via boardwalks and river journeys. Deer Cave is the world's largest cave passage and the Sarawak Chamber is the world's largest chamber at 700 m (2,297 ft) long, 300 m (984 ft) wide and 70 m (230 ft) high. The nightly exodus of millions of bats from Deer Cave is one of Borneo's great natural wonders. Accommodation includes dormitories, homestays and the Marriott Resort.

Left: In addition to exploring the caves of Gunung Mulu National Park, adventurous tourists can take river boat journeys, go rock climbing, jungle trekking, mountain biking or visit longhouses.

Chapter 4: East Malaysia, Sabah

Sabah is Malaysia's second largest state with Kota Kinabalu ('KK') the capital. Once known as Jesselton, it was damaged by Allied bombs at the end of World War II, then rebuilt and renamed Kota Kinabalu.

Kota Kinabalu and Beyond

This coastal city faces the South China Sea and its waterfront is lined with hotels, bars and cafés. Tunku Abdul Rahman Park consisting of five islands is situated just off the coast. Accommodation is available on some of the islands while Sapi is popular for snorkelling. Sutera Harbour, near the city centre includes two hotels, a marina, a golf course, restaurants and bars.

Above: Cultural performances by various ethnic communities are a must for all tourists.

Left: Gaya Street's Sunday market spreads along the main street and into several side streets.

Above: Malaysia's highest
peak, Mount Kinabalu at
4,101 m (13,455 ft) is located
in Sabah.

Left: Visitors to Sandakan can
see the house where Agnes Keith
wrote about her experiences of
living there in the 1930s in the
book 'Land Below the Wind',
then enjoy croquet and tea at the
English Tea House. Orphaned
Orang-utans can be seen in
Sepilok, while an elevated
walkway at the Rainforest
Discovery Centre (pictured) is
ideal for observing canopy plants.

Sabah - Natural Places and Parks

Sabah's national parks and natural areas are protected habitats for plants and animals. Visitors travel to Sabah to experience wild places like Kinabalu Park, Kinabatangan River, Tabin Wildlife Reserve, Maliau Basin, Danum Valley and Turtle Islands.

Above: Lahad Datu is the gateway for ecotourists travelling to the Danum Valley and Maliau Basin. Both have a 'lost world' setting with Maliau Basin being only 'discovered' in 1947 and first explored in 1988. In Danum Valley a canopy walk enables visitors to see wildlife that lives high above the rainforest floor.

Top right: Sepilok is home to orphaned Orang-utans.

Below right: Of the eight species of hornbills found on Borneo, the Oriental Pied Hornbill is the one most commonly seen.

This page: *Sabah's Kinabatangan River and its tributary, the Menanggul, are two of Borneo's best locations to spot wildlife. Ecotourists traverse both rivers in small boats and may see Proboscis Monkeys, Orang-utans, Bornean Pygmy Elephants, reptiles, and many bird species.*

Getting About

Malaysia is connected to the world via several international airports. Kuala Lumpur International Airport (KLIA) is the main gateway with secondary airports in Penang, Kuching and Kota Kinabalu. Some of the islands and other smaller airports accept flights from Singapore and Indonesia.

Six commercial airlines operate internationally and domestically within Malaysia – AirAsia, AirAsia X, Berjaya, Firefly, Malaysia Airlines and MASwings. The latter connects isolated communities in East Malaysia but has plans to fly regionally.

KTM operates trains within Malaysia with connecting services through to Thailand and Singapore. These trains provide sleepers on overnight journeys as well as seating in various classes. The luxurious Eastern and Oriental Express (E & O) connects Bangkok and Singapore via Malaysia with several monthly departures. Train enthusiasts can ride the only train on Borneo: it operates between Tanjung Aru (near Kota Kinabalu) and Tenom in Sabah. There's also the funicular railway to the summit of Penang Hill which makes an interesting ride.

Cruise ships visit various Malaysian ports, the principal ones being Port Klang, Penang, Langkawi and Kota Kinabalu. It is possible to travel to Malaysia by ferry from ports in Indonesia and into Sandakan from the Philippines. There are also ferries from Langkawi to southern Thailand.

The North South Highway travels the length of the West Coast with connections through to Singapore (crossings at the Causeway and Tuas) and into Thailand at Bukit Kayu Hitam in Kedah. There is also a crossing into Thailand at Rantau Panjang over the Golok River on the East Coast plus several other smaller crossings.

Right: Travelling around Kuala Lumpur is relatively easy by using public transport systems such as the monorail.

Malaysia has a good road and highway system including some toll roads, especially around Kuala Lumpur. Cars travel on the left-hand side of the road and most signs are in English. Buses and long-distance taxis connect major and smaller towns and provide a cost-effective form of travel for tourists. Boats also operate in the remotest parts of Malaysia.

Kuala Lumpur has a good public transport system of rail, monorail, taxis or the KL Hop-On Hop-Off Bus which visits the main sights.

Left: Malaysia has a good network of roads with many expressways and tollways throughout the country.

Above: Discerning travellers can enjoy the trip of a lifetime aboard the luxurious Eastern & Oriental Express that travels through Peninsular Malaysia on its journey from Singapore to Bangkok in Thailand.

Resources

Contacts

The following websites are useful for discovering more about Malaysia.

Asian Overland Services: www.asianoverland.com.my

Department of Wildlife and National Parks Peninsular
    Malaysia (PERHILITAN): www.wildlife.gov.my

Forest Department Sarawak/Sarawak National Parks:
    www.forestry.sarawak.gov.my

KTM Berhad (Malaysia Railway): ktmb.com.my

Malaysia F1 Grand Prix: www.malaysiangp.com.my

Monsoon Cup: www.monsooncup.com.my

Mountain Torq (via ferrata Mount Kinabalu):
    www.mountaintorq.com

Sabah Parks: www.sabahparks.org.my

Sabah Tourism: www.sabahtourism.com

Sarawak Tourism: www.sarawaktourism.com

Tourism Malaysia: www.tourism.gov.my

World Wide Fund for Nature Malaysia (WWF-Malaysia):
    www.wwf.org.my

Airlines

AirAsia (and AirAsia X): www.airasia.com

Berjaya Air: www.berjaya-air.com

Firefly: www.fireflyz.com.my

Malaysia Airlines: www.malaysiaairlines.com

MASwings: www.maswings.com.my

References

Bowden, D. 2000. *Globetrotter Visitor's Guide Taman
    Negara - Malaysia's Premier National Park*. New
    Holland Publishers.

Bowden, D. 2011. *Enchanting Borneo*. John Beaufoy
    Publishing.

Moore, W. and G. Cubitt. 2003. *This is Malaysia*. New
    Holland Publishers.

Phillipps, A. and F. Liew. 2000. *Globetrotters Visitor's
    Guide, Kinabalu Park, Sabah, Malaysian Borneo*. New
    Holland Publishers.

Prof. Dato' Dr Sham Sani (Editor). 1998. *The Encyclopedia
    of Malaysia: Volume 1, The Environment*. Archipelago
    Press.

Rathborne, A. B. 1898. *Camping and Tramping in Malaya
    – Fifteen Years' Pioneering in the Native States of the
    Malay Peninsula*. John Beaufoy Publishing.

Soepadmo, Dr E. (Editor). *The Encyclopedia of Malaysia:
    Volume 2, Plants*. Archipelago Press.

Acknowledgments

The author would like to thank Malaysia Tourism, Sabah
Tourism and Sarawak Tourism for their kind assistance.

The publishers and the author would like to express
special thanks to Ken Scriven for his advice and support
during the preparation of this book.

About the Author

David Bowden is a freelance photojournalist based in
Malaysia who specializes in travel and the environment.
While Australian, he's been in Asia for longer than he can
remember and returns to his home country as a tourist.
When he's not travelling the world, he enjoys relaxing with
his equally adventurous wife Maria and daughter Zoe. He
is also the author of two other books in this series,
Enchanting Borneo and *Enchanting Singapore*.

Index

First published in the United Kingdom in 2012 by John Beaufoy Publishing,
11 Blenheim Court, 316 Woodstock Road, Oxford OX2 7NS, England
www.johnbeaufoy.com

10 9 8 7 6 5 4 3 2 1

Copyright © 2012 John Beaufoy Publishing Limited
Copyright © 2012 in text David Bowden
The author asserts his moral rights to be identified as the author of this work.
Copyright © 2012 in photographs see below

All rights reserved. No part of this publication may be reproduced, stored in a retrieval system or transmitted in any form
or by any means, electronic, mechanical, photocopying, recording or otherwise, without the prior written permission of
the publishers and copyright holders. Great care has been taken to maintain the accuracy of the information contained in
this work. However, neither the publishers nor the author can be held responsible for any consequences arising from the
use of the information contained therein.

ISBN 978-1-906780-77-7

Designed by Glyn Bridgewater
Cartography by William Smuts
Project management by Rosemary Wilkinson

Printed and bound in Singapore by Tien Wah Press (Pte) Ltd.

All photographs © David Bowden except for:
Erik Fearn (p4-5, top); Sabah Tourism (p20 top); Sabah Tourism (p21 above); David Li (p24 bottom); Mountain Torq (p28);
Mandarin Oriental Hotel (p34); Traders Hotel (p35); Parkroyal Penang Resort (p47 top); Shangri-la Rasa Sayang Resort
(p47 bottom); Senai to Desaru Expressway (p52); Japamala Resort (p60, 61); Resorts World Genting (p65 bottom); S.K.
Chong (p67); Sarawak Tourism (p69, top); Sabah Tourism (p73, top).

Cover captions and credits:
Back cover (left to right): *Putrajaya mosque* © David Bowden;
James Brooke Restaurant, Kuching waterfront © David Bowden; *Pitcher plant* © David Bowden;
Tioman Island © David Bowden.
Front cover top (left to right): *Cheong Fatt Tze mansion in George Town, Penang* © David Bowden;
Malayan Tiger © David Bowden; *Bunga Raya, the national flower* © David Bowden;
A baby Orang-utan © David Bowden.
Front cover (centre): *Tea plantations at Cameron Highlands* © Shutterstock/Szefei.
Front cover (bottom): *The Petronas Twin Towers at night* © Mick Shippen.